# BODY CHANGES

## Christine Green

Wayland

*Also in paperback:*

Growing Into Sex

**Series editor:** Marcella Streets
**Series design:** Cooper-Wilson
**Consultants:** Dr Pramilla Senanayake and Dr John Coleman

First published in 1989 by
Wayland (Publishers) Ltd
61 Western Road, Hove
East Sussex BN3 1JD, England

This edition published in 1991 by
Wayland (Publishers) Ltd

**British Library Cataloguing in Publication Data**
Green, Christine
  Body changes.
  1. Man. Puberty
  I. Title   II. Series
  612'.661

ISBN 0-7502-0256-4

Phototypeset by DP Press, Sevenoaks
Printed in Italy by G. Canale C.S.p.A., Turin
Bound in Belgium by Casterman S.A.

# Contents

# From Child into Adolescent

Our bodies are growing and constantly changing throughout life but never more so than during adolescence. Adolescence is the time between childhood and adulthood. It lasts for several years, usually from around the age of ten to nineteen. It is an exciting time of life but it can also be difficult. The vast number of physical changes can leave you feeling awkward, clumsy and as if you do not 'belong' in your new, adult form. You may be worried that you are not developing properly or at the right pace, or that your appearance is unattractive.

In addition to the physical changes, you may find your moods changing: one day you might be bursting with energy, the next you may want to spend alone in your bedroom.

Mood changes during adolescence are common. Some days you may feel like jumping with joy, others you may want to spend alone in your room.

*Parents may find it difficult to cope with your new-found independence.*

While all these feelings are perfectly normal, they can be very confusing. On top of all this, your relationship with your parents will be altering: they may expect you to behave like an adult but still treat you as a child. You yourself may want to be independent and grown up but at the same time worry about how you will cope with the responsibility of becoming an adult. You may wish you were a child again.

This series of books aims to help you through this time. Finding out exactly what is happening to your body and how this affects your moods will help you feel more confident during your teenage years. You will discover that everyone experiences worries and fears but that they can be overcome.

This book concentrates mainly on what happens to your body during adolescence. These changes are called 'puberty'. Other books in the series cover sex, moods and feelings, family and friends, diet and health and teenage parenthood.

Remember to read about body changes for both sexes, as it is important to understand what your friends of the opposite sex are going through.

# From Child into Adolescent

## WHEN DOES PUBERTY START?

Puberty usually begins somewhere between the ages of ten and thirteen for most girls, and between eleven and fourteen for boys. However there can be very wide variations in this. Some girls may start developing as early as eight years old and others not until they are sixteen.

## WHAT HAPPENS DURING PUBERTY?

There are two major types of physical development during puberty, sexual changes and body changes.

Sexual changes are those necessary for having children, for example the growth of the womb in girls. Body changes include those that are not necessary for parenthood, like the development of underarm hair.

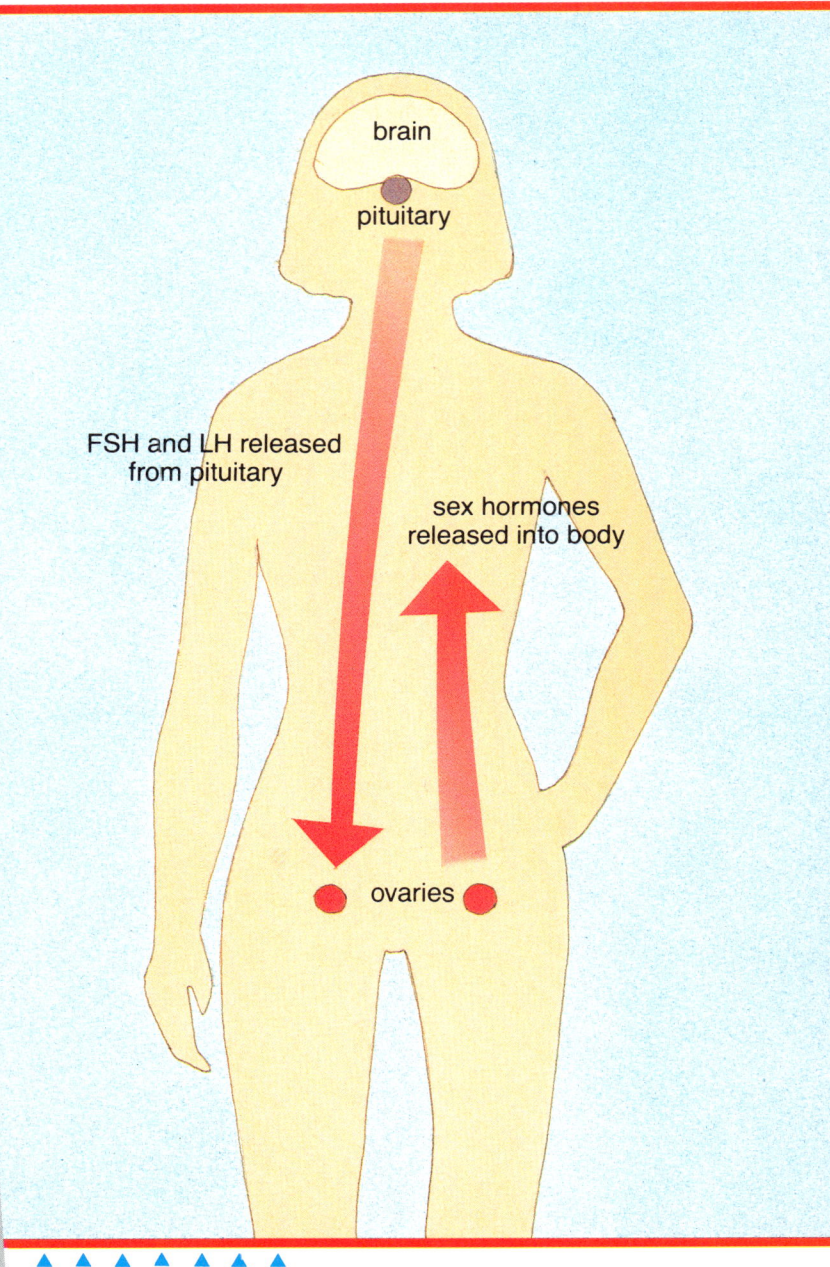

brain

pituitary

FSH and LH released from pituitary

sex hormones released into body

ovaries

**Above** The body changes that occur during adolescence are triggered by changes in the level of hormones.
**Left** The age at which puberty begins varies widely.

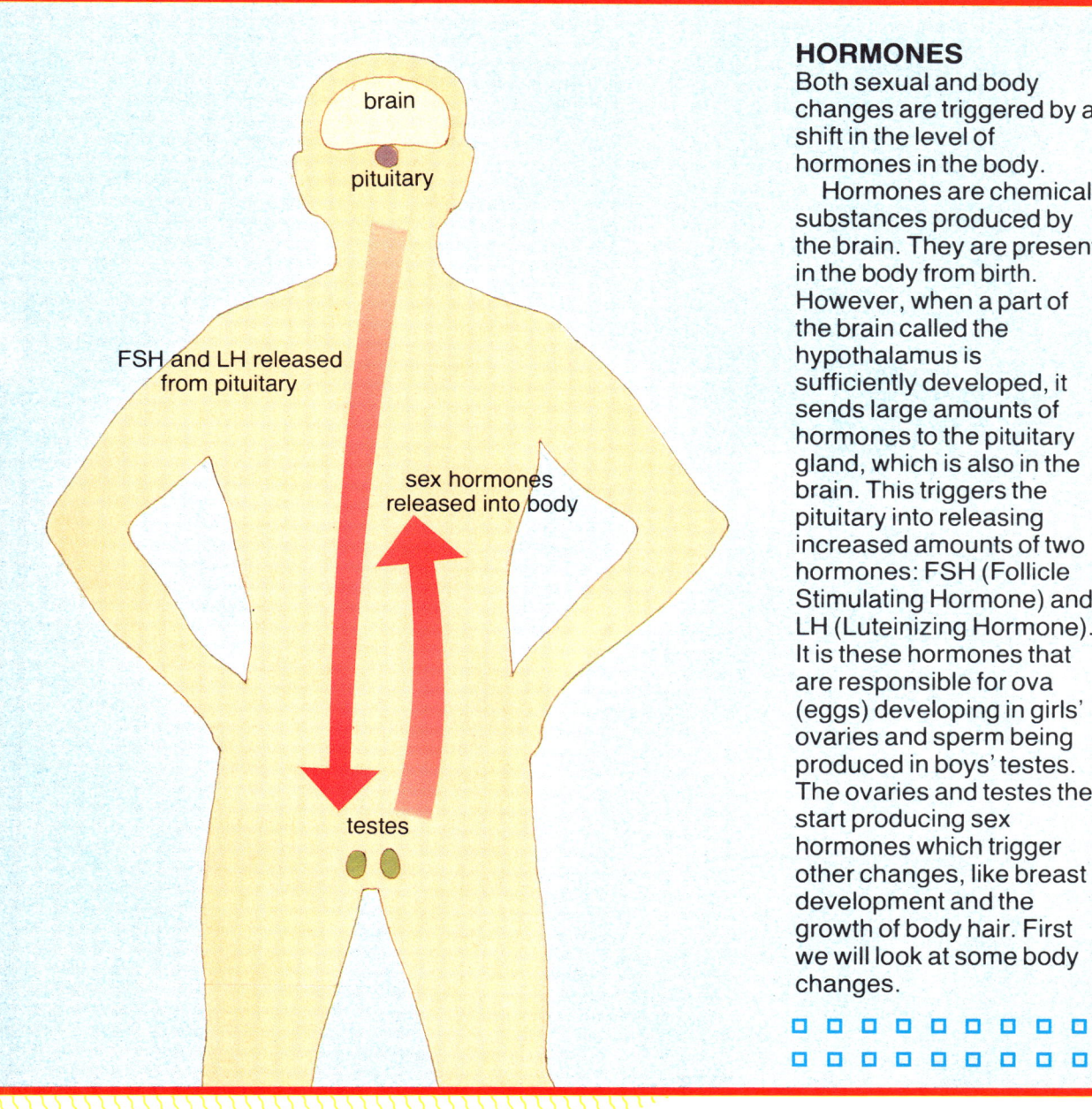

brain

pituitary

FSH and LH released
from pituitary

sex hormones
released into body

testes

## HORMONES

Both sexual and body changes are triggered by a shift in the level of hormones in the body.

Hormones are chemical substances produced by the brain. They are present in the body from birth. However, when a part of the brain called the hypothalamus is sufficiently developed, it sends large amounts of hormones to the pituitary gland, which is also in the brain. This triggers the pituitary into releasing increased amounts of two hormones: FSH (Follicle Stimulating Hormone) and LH (Luteinizing Hormone). It is these hormones that are responsible for ova (eggs) developing in girls' ovaries and sperm being produced in boys' testes. The ovaries and testes then start producing sex hormones which trigger other changes, like breast development and the growth of body hair. First we will look at some body changes.

# Height and Shape

The first changes you will experience during puberty are probably a sudden increase in height and changes in your shape.

The first parts of the body to increase in size are the feet and hands, followed by the arms and legs, which get a bit longer.

## HEIGHT

Girls generally begin puberty at a younger age than boys and so, around the age of eight to eleven years old, they grow much taller. Boys go through this 'growth spurt' roughly two years later.

The age at which you experience this is not an indication of how tall you will be as an adult. That depends partly on your parents' height, your health and nutrition.

During early puberty, girls tend to be taller than boys but by the time boys have reached the age of fourteen, they have normally caught up with, or overtaken, girls. On average girls have reached roughly their adult height by the time they are seventeen years old, but boys carry on growing until they are about nineteen. Growing does not stop completely at that stage: both boys and girls continue to grow just a few millimetres more during the following years.

## SHAPE

Both boys and girls gain weight and change shape during puberty. Girls will become aware that their hips are broadening and breasts beginning to develop. As they grow, boys' shoulders become broader and their muscles develop. Although it sounds terrifying, all these changes are gradual and probably more noticeable to you than anyone else.

**Average heights for boys and girls**

136 cm — Age 10

138 cm

153 cm — Age 13

157 cm

## FACE SHAPE

Although you may not be aware of it, your face gradually changes into a more adult shape during puberty. The nose and jaw become a bit more prominent and the hairline draws further back. Don't worry: it is something that takes time and alters with the rest of your body.

*Left* Your face gradually becomes more adult in shape during adolescence.

## VOICE

Boys will notice that their voice changes pitch during early adolescence, becoming 'broken' (slightly croaky) and then deeper. This happens because the larynx (voice box) grows along with the rest of the body.

★ ★ ★ ★ ★ ★ ★ ★ ★

*Below* There are many different sizes of people and types of body shape.

175 cm

Age 19

163 cm

## TYPES OF SHAPE

There are many different body shapes. While diet and exercise affect your weight, they cannot totally remodel your basic body shape. This does not mean that there is no point eating healthily and exercising, but that you should accept that you have a particular type of frame. If you are worried about how you feel about your body, see the chapter on worries and fears in this book and also *Diet and Health* and *Moods and Feelings* in this series.

# Body Hair

The hormone changes responsible for your increase in height and developing figure also trigger hair growth on various parts of the body – around your sexual organs, under your arms, on your face, arms and legs.

The amount of hair that grows varies enormously and so does the age at which it starts to grow, although this is usually between the ages of nine and eighteen. Dark hair shows up more than fair hair, of course. Although underarm and pubic hair is soft and sparse to begin with, it gradually becomes coarser and thicker as you get older. It may also be a different colour from the hair on your head. (You can read about hair on your head in the chapter on skin, hair and hygiene.)

## PUBIC HAIR

Pubic hair grows around the external sexual organs. Girls' pubic hair usually appears on the labia (outer lips of the vagina) first and then spreads up to form a triangular shape. Boys' pubic hair normally grows about the penis first and then around and below the testes.

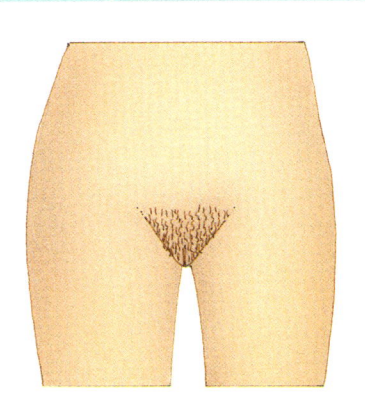 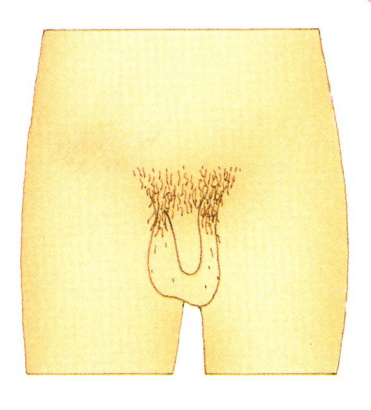

*Above* Girls' pubic hair.   *Above* Boys' pubic hair.

## UNDERARM HAIR

About a year or two after your pubic hair begins to grow around the genitals, hair starts to develop under your arms. At first it is sparse and fine but eventually it will get darker, coarser and thicker.

## BODY HAIR

Boys usually have more body hair than girls and it is usually coarser. Both boys and girls get hair growth on their arms and legs during puberty, however. Hair may also grow on your chest and abdomen later on in puberty (particularly in boys). The odd hair might also appear on your shoulders, back of the hands and on the feet. These are usually sparse – you are not going to turn into a gorilla!

## GIRLS AND FACIAL HAIR

Most people's faces are covered in fine hairs. Some of these may be dark and therefore more noticeable, especially above your top lip. This does not make girls unfeminine. If you feel embarrassed, the hair can be lightened with special cream bleach from a chemist (see below). Hairy eyebrows can be plucked into a neat shape with tweezers if you are unhappy with them. Do not pluck the hair from above the brow, as this will ruin the shape. Just pull out the straggly hairs below the main line of hair.

Girls' facial hair can be removed with tweezers (*right*) or bleached (*centre*).

**Below** Boys can shave off unwanted facial hair or pluck out stray hairs.

## BOYS AND FACIAL HAIR

Boys usually develop more hair on their faces than girls do. Hair first appears above the boy's top lip, then on his cheeks and chin. Like pubic and underarm hair, it is soft to start with but eventually coarsens. If you feel embarrassed, you can shave off the hair or pull out stray ones with tweezers.

# Body hair

## HAIR REMOVAL

Many people are happy with their bodily hair growth. However, you can remove it if you want to. If you feel that you have an unnatural amount of body hair, see your doctor. It may be that you have a hormone imbalance which can be put right.

When removing hair, always follow product instructions very carefully.

## BLEACHING

Hair can be made less noticeable with bleach, which can be reapplied when dark hair grows through. Do not use household bleach but a special cream bleach from a chemist.

## WAXING

Liquid wax is spread onto the hair and then ripped off when it has hardened, taking the hair with it. This can be painful and is best suited to leg hair. It can be done by an expert at a beauty salon or by yourself, using a kit at home.

## SHAVING

Electric shavers are easiest and safest to use. If you use a wet-shave razor, be careful not to cut yourself. Unfortunately hair often looks coarser when it grows back after having been shaved, so bear this in mind. Girls should avoid shaving their facial hair, pubic hair and thighs, as regrowth can be itchy and stubbly.

## DEPILATORY CREAMS

Depilatory cream or foam is spread onto the skin and left for a few minutes. When you wash it off, the hairs wash away too. If you use this method on your face, make sure you use a cream especially made for this. Never leave the cream on longer than recommended by the manufacturer, as this can harm your skin.

*Shaving leg hair makes regrowth feel coarse.*

# Sexual Changes: Girls

Around the age of nine or ten, a young girl will notice her body is beginning to alter. There may well be a slight weight increase, the hips begin to widen, the upper thighs become plumper, the waist takes shape and the breasts begin to develop.

## BREASTS

The main job of breasts is the production of milk in order to feed any babies a woman might have. They are also sexually attractive and sensitive to touch.

As breasts grow and develop, some girls may find them a little uncomfortable. One may even grow slightly faster than the other – very few women have breasts which are exactly the same size. At around the age of seventeen, the breasts will generally have reached their adult size.

**Body changes in girls**

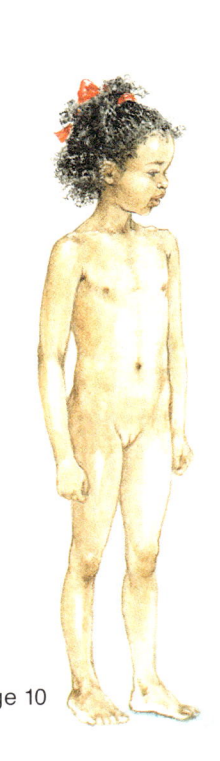

Age 10

Age 11-16

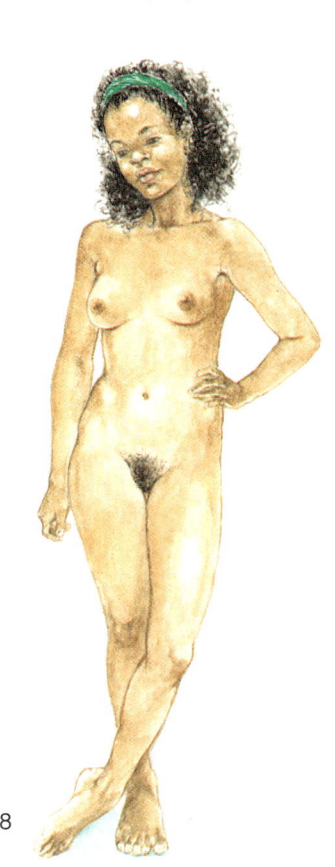

Age 17-28

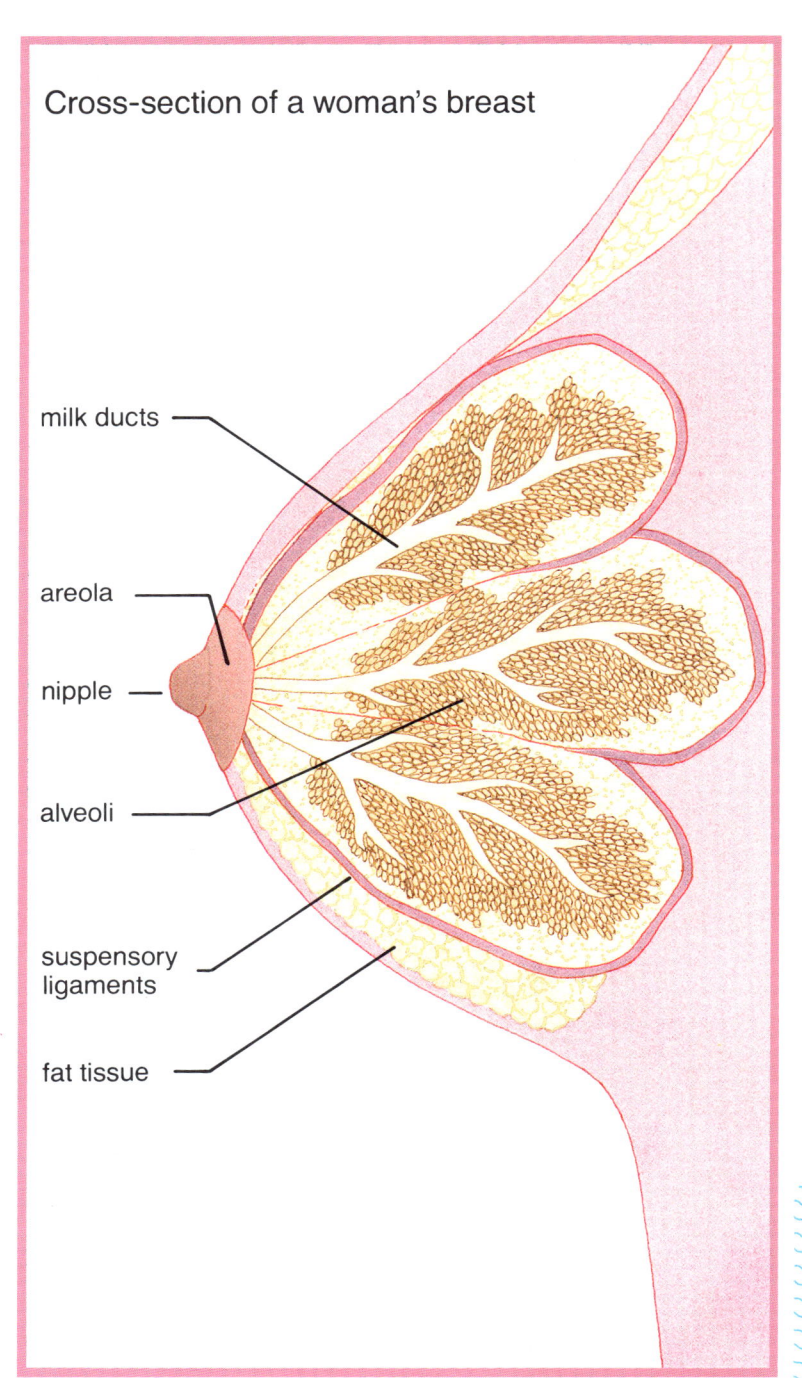

Cross-section of a woman's breast

milk ducts

areola

nipple

alveoli

suspensory ligaments

fat tissue

## HOW ARE BREASTS FORMED?

Each breast is made up of very many small glands and fatty tissue. The fat in breasts acts as a cushion for the milk ducts. It also determines the size of your breasts. All sizes of breast can feed a baby and are equally sensitive.

The most sensitive part of the breast is the nipple and, when aroused by being touched, the small surrounding muscles cause it to become erect (stand out). The area around the nipple (the areola) varies in colour from pink to very dark brown. It turns darker during puberty and also enlarges. The tiny lumps in it are glands.

The only natural support breasts have lies in the suspensory ligaments. These are thin bands of elastic-like tissue which run from the breast walls through the breast tissue itself. These tend to stretch as you get older, making the breasts droop.

## WEARING A BRA

Many girls like to wear bras but there is no medical reason for this. The weight of heavy breasts can stretch the suspensory ligaments and make the breasts droopy, though, and wearing a bra might help prevent this happening when you are young. Once stretched, they will not return to their former shape.

To find out a girl's bra size you need two measurements. First measure around the chest under the breasts and add 12cm. This is the bra size. Then measure around the chest at the level of the nipples. Take the first number away from the second measurement: the difference tells you the cup size.

- No difference – an A cup is required
- 2.5cm difference means a B cup
- 5 cm difference means a C cup
- 7.5cm difference means a D cup
- 10 cm difference means a DD cup
- 11.5cm difference means an E cup

## BOYS DEVELOPING BREASTS

Both boys and girls have the same hormones in their bodies, though in different amounts. In other words, although boys produce mainly male sex hormones, they also produce low levels of female sex hormones. Similarly girls have low levels of male sex hormones. Because of the sudden surge of hormones during puberty, occasionally boys might find a slight breast development. This will not last and will disappear as soon as the sex hormones have settled. If you are ever worried about what is going on in your body, ask a doctor or trustworthy adult.

## GIRLS' EXTERNAL SEX ORGANS

The external sex organs, those visible on the outside of the body, are called genitals. It is a good idea to examine these organs in privacy. Girls can use a mirror to look at theirs. Everybody's genitals are different in shape, size and colour, just as their faces are, so don't worry if yours aren't identical to your friends'.

## PUBIC MOUND

The triangular area between the legs and above the genitals is called the pubic mound. Made up of fatty tissue, it covers and helps protect the pubic bones underneath.

## OUTER LABIA

The outer lips of the vagina, closed around the inner lips, are called labia. They protect the other external sex organs. During puberty the labia become thicker and rounder, with hair growing around them.

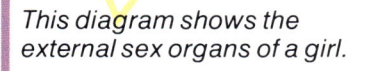

*This diagram shows the external sex organs of a girl.*

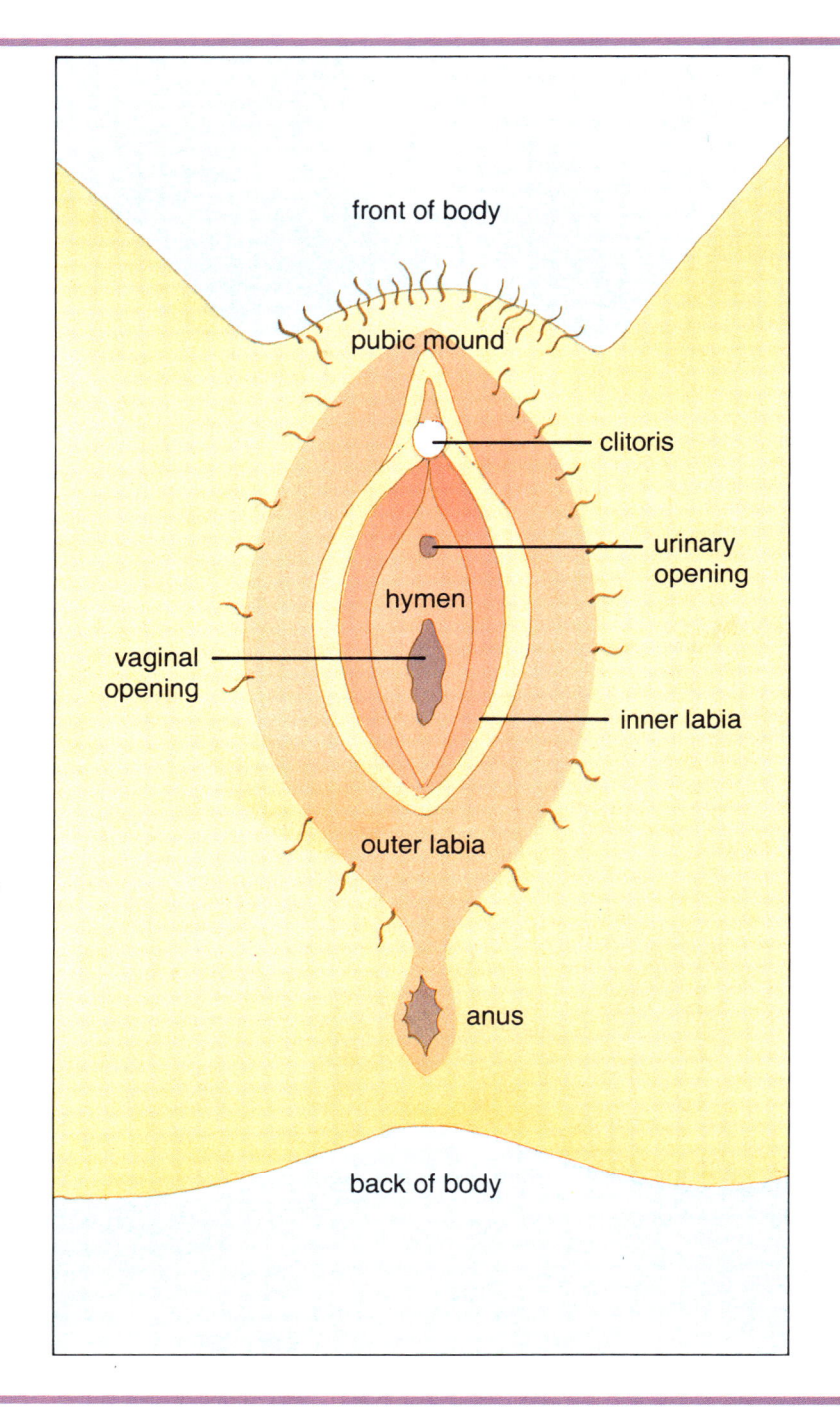

front of body

pubic mound

clitoris

urinary opening

hymen

vaginal opening

inner labia

outer labia

anus

back of body

## INNER LABIA

When the outer labia are parted, there are two thinner, far more delicate folds of skin called the inner labia, which are extremely sensitive to touch. Sometimes the inner labia stick out between the outer labia. When sexually excited, the inner labia swell slightly, change colour and also increase in size.

## CLITORIS

Amongst these inner folds is a small organ, about the size of a pea and the nerve centre of a girl's sexual feelings. It is covered by a fold of skin and is only just visible. During sexual arousal, blood rushes to the blood vessels in the clitoris, making it look red, and giving the girl a feeling of pleasure.

## VAGINAL OPENING

The opening to the vagina is shaped rather like a small concertina and leads to the internal sex organs from the outside of the body. Blood comes out of here when you have a period. Although small, it is so elastic that it is able to stretch to accommodate a penis during sex or a baby's head during childbirth.

## ANUS

The hole through which solid waste matter leaves your body when you go to the toilet.

## URINARY OPENING

The hole through which a girl passes urine.

## HYMEN

The entrance leading from the vagina into the body is partially blocked by a thin layer of skin called the hymen. As you grow, it gradually breaks; often it is torn during physical exercise or when inserting a tampon during a period. This does not hurt and can happen without you noticing. Sometimes the hymen breaks during a girl's first experience of sexual intercourse. However, a broken hymen does not mean that a girl has had sex.

## GIRLS' INTERNAL SEXUAL ORGANS

The internal sex organs of a girl are those that produce eggs to make babies, cause periods and house a baby during pregnancy. Like the rest of the body during puberty, the internal sex organs grow rapidly. They are protected by the bones in the pelvis.

In the section on internal sexual organs, we saw how the vagina led from the outside of the body to the sexual organs inside. In fact, the vagina leads to the cervix. This is often called the 'neck of the womb', because it joins the vagina to the womb.

## UTERUS

The uterus is the name given to the womb. Shaped like an upside-down pear, it is the place in which a baby grows during pregnancy. Each month, from puberty until the menopause (the time when a woman can no longer have children), the lining of the uterus gets thicker, ready for a fertilized egg to embed itself and grow into a baby. If the egg is not fertilized, it disintegrates. The thickened lining of the uterus breaks down and passes out of the vagina in blood as a period.

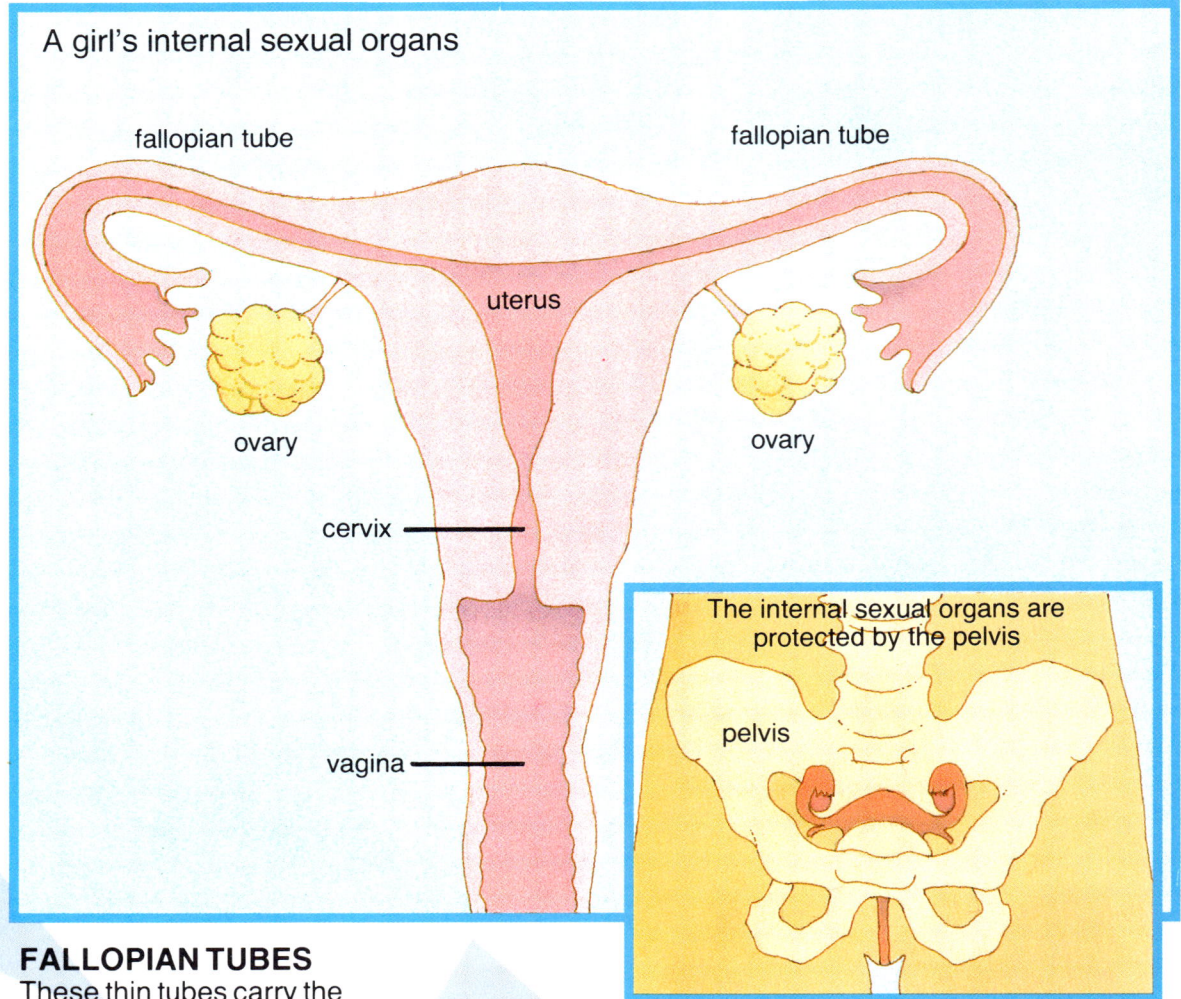

A girl's internal sexual organs

fallopian tube

fallopian tube

uterus

ovary

ovary

cervix

vagina

The internal sexual organs are protected by the pelvis

pelvis

## FALLOPIAN TUBES

These thin tubes carry the eggs from the ovaries to the womb. It is while an egg is in these tubes that a girl can become pregnant if she has sex and a male sperm fertilizes the egg. The fertilized egg then travels to the uterus and attaches itself to the lining. (See *Growing Into Sex* in this series for more information on sex and pregnancy.)

## OVARIES

Ovaries contain the egg cells necessary to produce a baby. Girls have two ovaries. They are just outside the womb but connected to it by small fibres.

Girls have a lifetime store of eggs (about 400,000) in their ovaries from birth. During puberty hormones make the ovaries release these eggs. Normally one egg is released each month from alternate ovaries. This happens until the menopause, which is when periods stop, at around the age of fifty.

# Sexual Changes: Boys

For a boy it is obvious that his external sex organs are growing, as they are more easily visible than those of a girl. First the testes start to grow, followed by the penis about a year later. Boys will also notice that they have more frequent erections. (An erection is when the penis is hard and stands up.) See the chapter on worries and fears for more on erections and wet dreams.

## TESTES

About the size of small plums, the left one usually hanging lower than the right, the testes produce the sperm necessary to fertilize a girl's egg and make babies. They also make the hormones that create body changes like beard growth.

From puberty onwards boys continually produce millions of sperm. This continues into old age. It is within the testes that the sperm are stored.

**Body changes in boys**

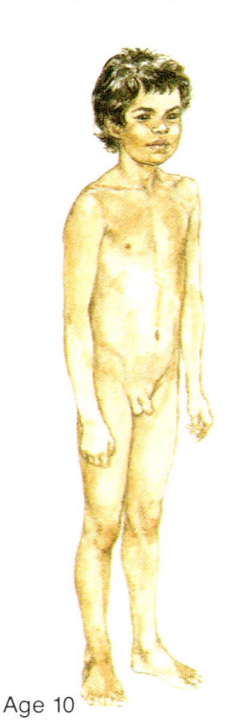
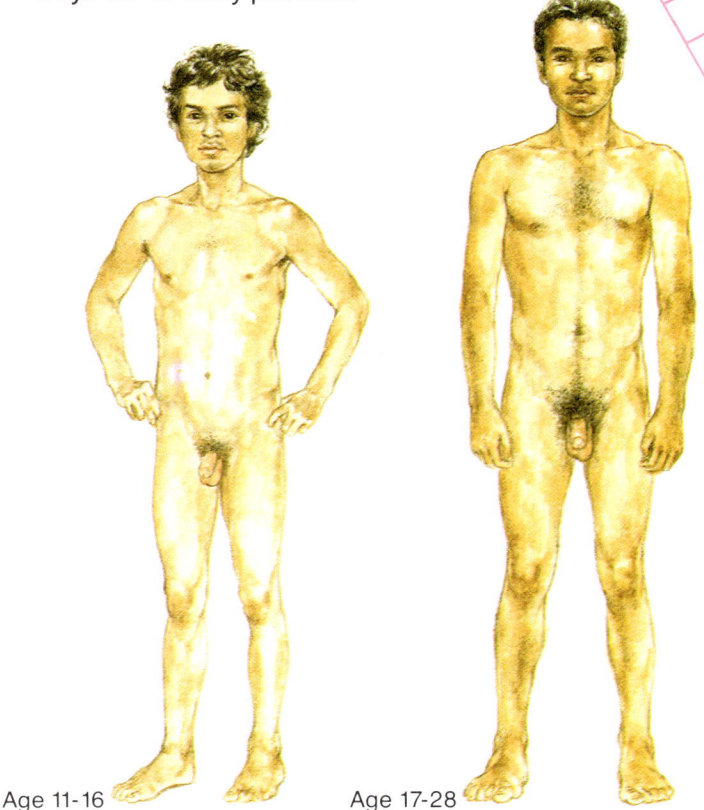

Age 10          Age 11-16          Age 17-28

# Sexual Changes: Boys

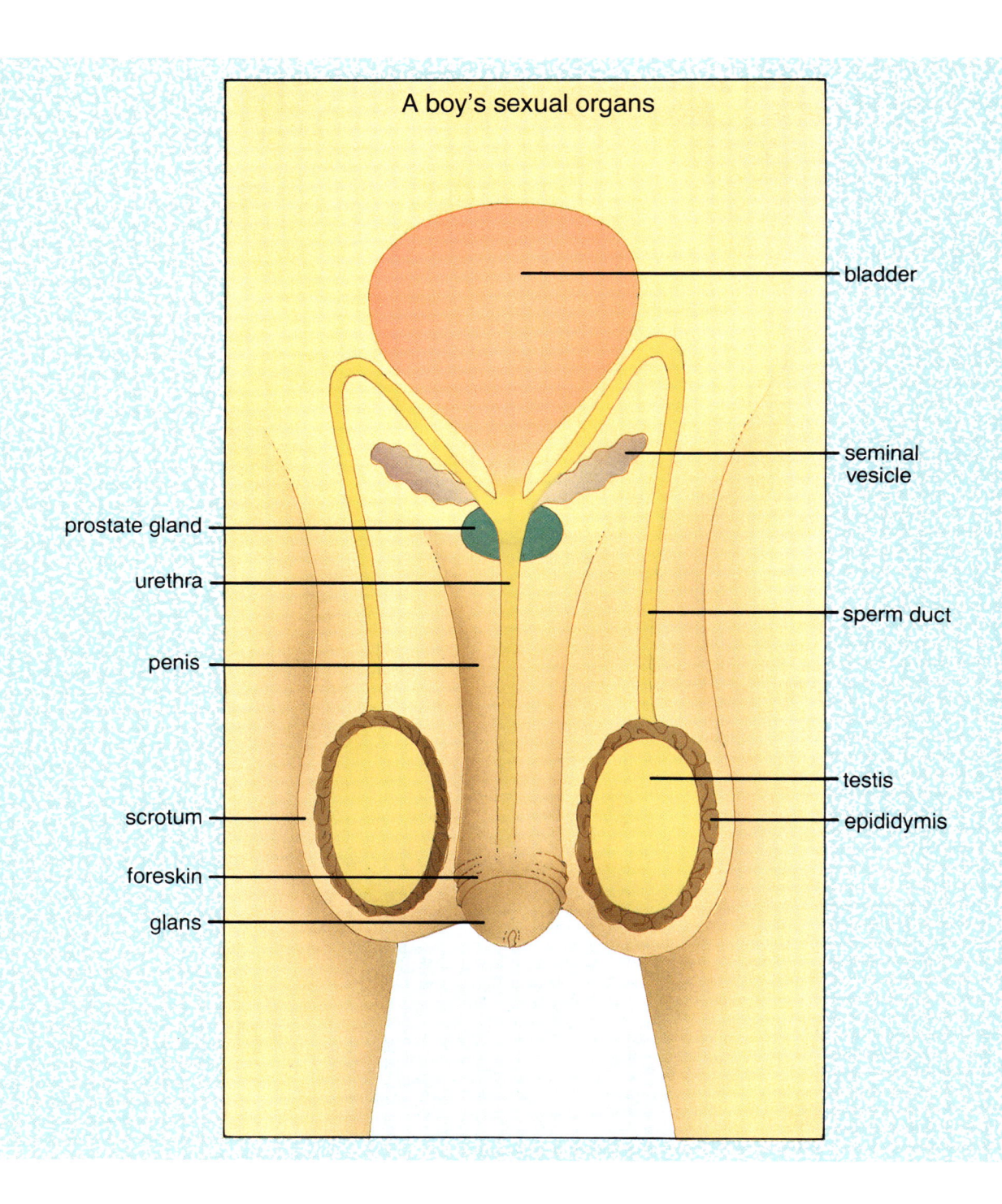

A boy's sexual organs

bladder

seminal vesicle

prostate gland

urethra

penis

scrotum

foreskin

glans

sperm duct

testis

epididymis

## SCROTUM

The scrotum is the loose pocket of wrinkly skin that guards the testes. Sperm can only be produced at a temperature lower than that inside the body, so the testes are held outside the body in the scrotum. However, when the scrotum is exposed to cold temperatures it shrinks, drawing the testes closer to the body for warmth.

## EPIDIDYMIS

Sperm cells are pushed from the testes into a coiled tube (called an epididymis) at the back of each testis. It is responsible for maturing the sperm cells.

## SPERM DUCTS

These tubes carry sperm from the epididymis to the urethra, past the seminal vesicles and prostate gland.

## SEMINAL VESICLES

These glands, attached to the sperm ducts, provide a fluid which gives sperm energy on their journey.

## PROSTATE GLAND

This gland produces the fluid in which the sperm move.

## URETHRA

Boys' urethras have two jobs: to carry urine out of the body and carry sperm in a fluid called semen. This liquid comes from the seminal vesicles and prostate gland during the sperm's journey from the epididymis. A valve closes off to prevent sperm and urine leaving the penis at the same time.

## FORESKIN

This is the loose, darker-coloured sleeve of skin which lies over the glans to protect it. In childhood, the foreskin is actually attached to the glans but over a number of years it loosens and eventually moves over the glans quite easily.

In some countries and within certain cultures, it is the custom to cut the foreskin a few days after birth. This is called circumcision. This is sometimes done for hygienic reasons, as dirt can gather under the foreskin and cause infections. These can be avoided by rolling back the foreskin and washing under it regularly.

## PENIS

The penis is roughly cylinder-shaped and is on the outside of the body above the testes. It is usually soft and hangs limp. When sexually aroused or excited, an increase in blood-flow to it makes it stand up, hard and erect, so that it can fit into a girl's vagina. This is called an erection. The most sensitive part of the penis, which is full of nerve endings, is the tip called the glans.

# Periods

One of the major events of puberty is the start of a girl's periods. This marks her ability to have children (although it is possible to become pregnant before a first period). Some girls feel excited and proud that their periods have started but others feel embarrassed and worried that this will stop them playing sports. This need not be the case, especially if they use tampons (see below).

### WHAT IS A PERIOD?

As you read earlier, a period happens when an unfertilized egg is rejected by a girl's uterus, together with the womb lining and blood. The blood trickles out of the vagina over a few days and, although it looks more, is usually only a few tablespoonfuls in total. The blood can be caught in a specially bought sanitary towel, tampon or home-made cloth pad. A period lasts between two and eight days. Boys do not have periods.

### MYTHS

In the past some people believed having a period was the body's way of ridding itself of evil spirits. The Romans blamed menstruating women for blighting their crops and in Persia (now Iran), if periods went on longer than four days, the women were flogged in the belief that it was a sure sign of them being corrupt.

Some people believed menstrual blood had magical properties, such as the ability to cure epilepsy; there were tribes who believed the mere presence of a menstruating woman could protect against storms. Some myths have lingered, especially the one that washing one's hair during a period is harmful. This is not true. Periods are perfectly normal and should not be treated as an illness. Girls can behave exactly as normal, including bathing and swimming.

*It is a myth that girls should not swim when they have their periods.*

## WHEN DO PERIODS START?

Although no one can say exactly when a girl is going to begin her periods, they normally start between the ages of nine and eighteen. As a general rule, they normally commence midway through puberty, with the average age in Britain, for example, being around eleven years.

## WHAT ARE THE SIGNS?

In the past, starting periods was seen as a cause for celebration. Even in the twentieth century, the start of a young girl's periods is still a noteworthy event in her life. Normally a white discharge from the vagina is a sure sign that a girl's body is adapting for a period in about a month or so. She may also feel a dull, heavy ache around her lower abdomen. A first period is often brownish in colour.

## THE MENSTRUAL CYCLE

Menstruation is another word for periods. The 'menstrual cycle' means the number of days between the first days of your periods. There are on average four weeks between the beginning of one period and the beginning of the next, but different women's cycles vary from twenty to thirty-five days. Some people like to keep a note of their period dates, so they can check their cycle length and know roughly when their period is due.

This is how the cycle progresses: every 28 days or so (the time varies), the pituitary gland sends a

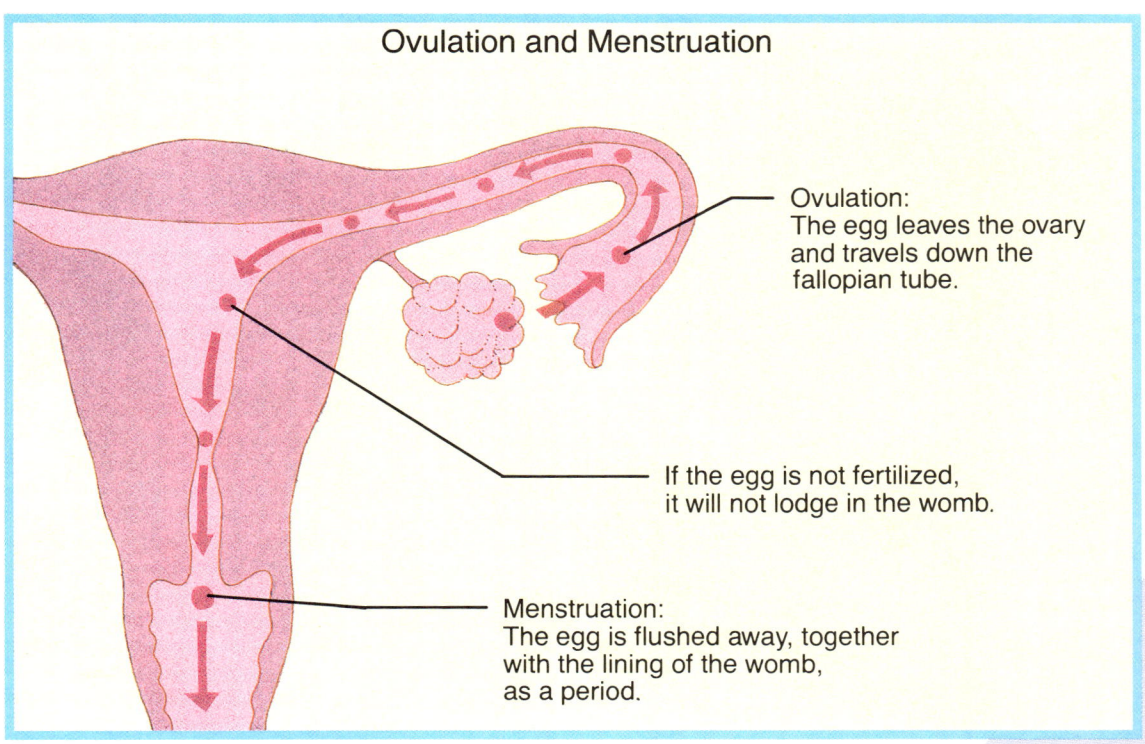

### Ovulation and Menstruation

Ovulation:
The egg leaves the ovary and travels down the fallopian tube.

If the egg is not fertilized, it will not lodge in the womb.

Menstruation:
The egg is flushed away, together with the lining of the womb, as a period.

▶ ▶ ▶ ▶ message to the ovaries telling them to ripen an egg. As you read earlier, the egg then makes its journey towards the uterus via the fallopian tubes. This is called ovulation and is the most likely time to get pregnant. Ovulation occurs mid-way between periods. If a couple have sexual intercourse without contraception, then the egg may become fertilized with a boy's sperm and fix itself securely on the lining of the uterus. However, if fertilization has not taken place, then the uterus lining (which has thickened in preparation for the possibility of a fertilized egg) breaks up, and a period starts.

## WHAT AFFECTS PERIODS?

Periods may be affected by a great many things: worry over exams or excitement can either cause a period to be late or to be missed altogether. A girl's first few periods may be rather light, and there may be several months between them. They will settle down eventually, although it may take a year or so.

## COPING WITH DISCOMFORT

Some girls may have discomfort during a period, such as a dragging pain, tiredness, feeling bloated or faint. Painkillers, a hot bath and a hot-water bottle held against the stomach can help relieve period pain. Some people find regular exercise helps ease it too.

## PROBLEMS WITH PERIODS

Men are fortunate in that their sex hormones remain pretty even all the time but for women the hormonal cycle is not so simple. The hormones which are carried around in a girl's bloodstream can affect other parts of her body, causing her to feel slightly unwell, or irritable, before and during a period.

✳ ✳ ✳ ✳ ✳ ✳ ✳ ✳

**Left** *Worry over exams or school work can make a period late or cause it to be missed altogether.*

**Right** *Some girls find that regular exercise helps reduce pain during periods.*

◁
◁ *A hot-water bottle can help*
◁ *ease stomach cramps.*

### DYSMENORRHOEA (PAINFUL PERIODS)

Until recently this condition was not taken seriously by doctors. However, hormones are now generally thought to be the cause. They are responsible for releasing prostaglandin, which causes the muscles of the uterus to contract, rather like a miniature version of labour. The symptoms of dysmenorrhoea include bloatedness, a feeling of nausea, irritability and, perhaps more commonly, painful cramps around the pelvic area, sometimes spreading around the back and down the legs.

There is a lot that can be done to lessen this discomfort. Doctors can prescribe an anti-prostaglandin drug which works by preventing too much prostaglandin being released into the body. If the pain is not bad enough to warrant a visit to the doctor, then bed-rest with a hot-water bottle over the painful area and a painkiller work wonders.

### AMENORRHOEA (NO PERIODS)

In most cases this is related to a hormonal type of disorder, or the fact that the sufferer may be underweight or dieting too hard (see *Diet and Health* in this series). It is quite normal for a fourteen-year-old not to be menstruating and doctors would be unlikely to investigate further until the girl was at least seventeen years old.

## PMT (PREMENSTRUAL TENSION)

Until relatively recently, this was considered to be a psychological problem but thankfully doctors are beginning to realize that this is not the case. Although PMT is a whole collection of different symptoms, varying from one girl to another, the most frequently listed symptoms are: headaches, clumsiness, depression, tearfulness, weight-gain, insomnia, bloatedness, tender breasts and tiredness. Of course no two girls will have exactly the same problems and indeed some might have them all and more! Doctors believe that PMT is related to hormones. It is a good idea to keep a diary each month of when your symptoms occur and then, after several months, go along to a doctor, who will be able to offer advice.

Although periods are nicknamed 'the curse', there is no need for girls to suffer silently; if the pain or symptoms are making a girl's life miserable, she should definitely seek advice from a doctor.

## SANITARY PROTECTION

Before a girl's periods even begin, she needs to think about some form of sanitary protection (something used to catch blood from periods).

Many girls use towels or pads, mainly because their mothers have recommended them, but tampons are equally popular. In countries where these are not available or are very expensive, many women make their own sanitary protection in the form of linen squares which are folded, stitched and held in place with a cloth belt. They can be washed and used again.

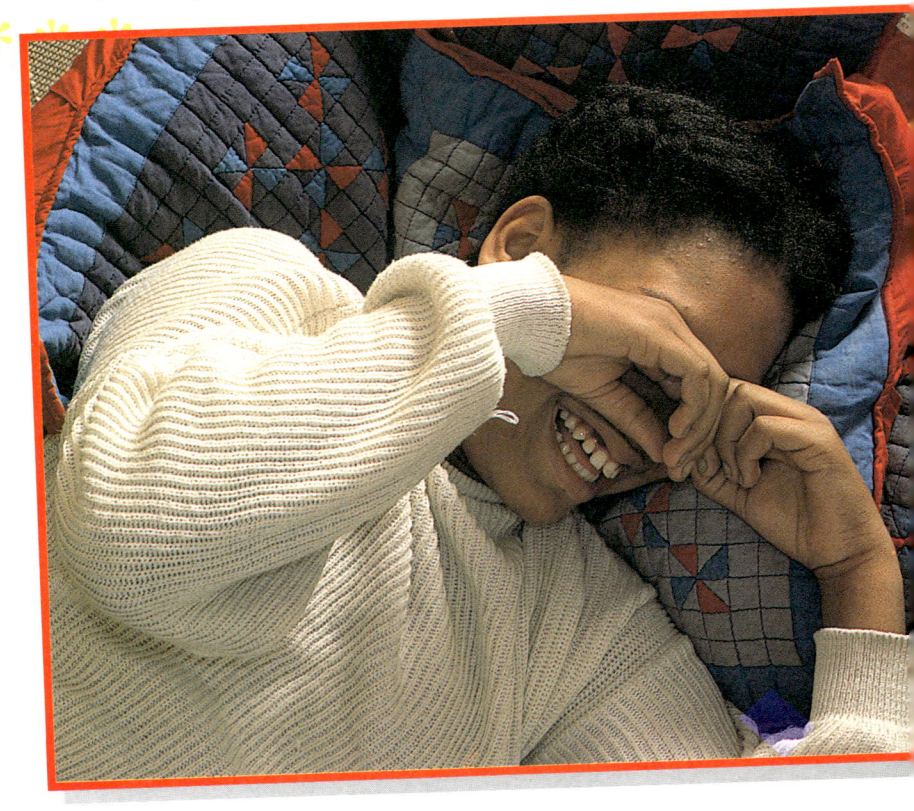

*Crying, depression and tiredness before periods may be symptoms of premenstrual tension.*

# Periods

## TOWELS

Available in many shapes and sizes, sanitary towels or pads are still extremely popular, despite a growing trend towards wearing tampons. There are basically two types of towel, both of which come in varying sizes and thicknesses, to match the heaviness of a period. Looped towels are suspended from a special sanitary belt, which is worn around the waist. Stick-on towels have a strip of adhesive which is attached to ordinary pants.

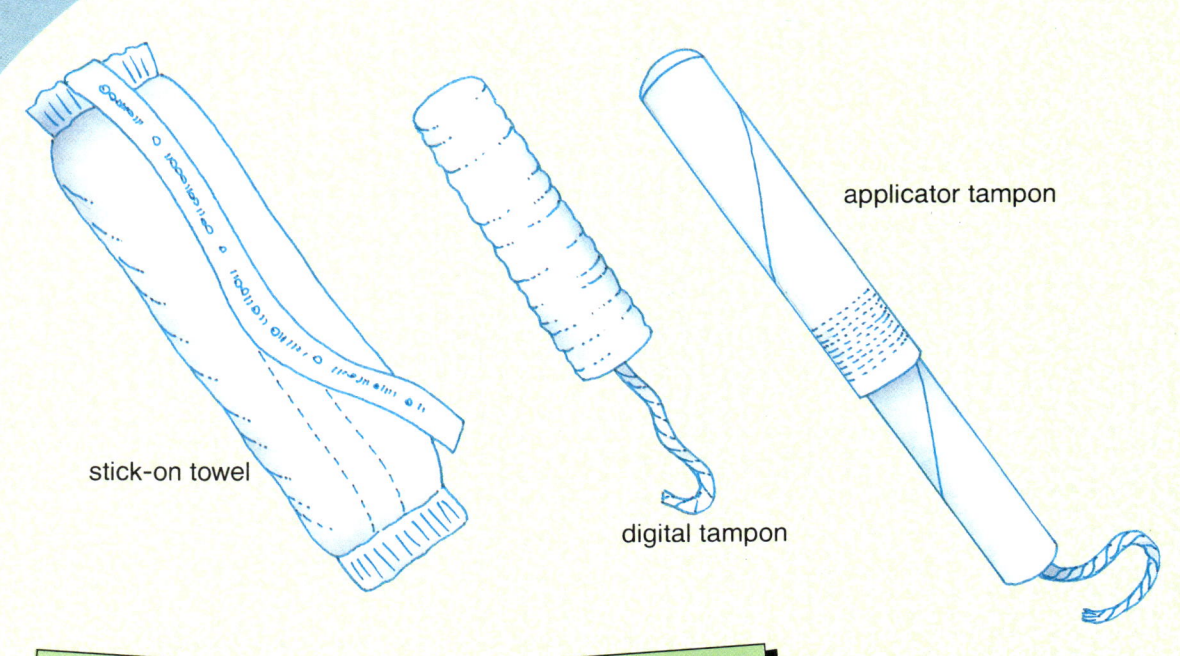

stick-on towel

digital tampon

applicator tampon

## TAMPONS

Many young girls wear tampons during their periods. There are two sorts of tampon, digital and applicator.

## DIGITAL

This tampon is a pad of compressed absorbent material. It may be inserted into the vagina using a clean finger.

## APPLICATOR

This is not as compressed as the digital tampon because it has an applicator, made of two cardboard tubes, with which to insert it. For girls who perhaps are worried about how to insert a tampon, this may be the best one for them to try first.

## HOW TO INSERT A TAMPON

The first time a girl inserts a tampon may seem rather odd and she may find herself tensing up in case it hurts, but the secret is to relax:

- Hands should always be washed before and after inserting a tampon.
- Tampons are bought in different absorbencies, from regular blood flow through to heavy. The regular size is usually the smallest. The smallest-sized tampon should be tried first: a larger size can be used later if necessary.
- Relax. Squatting, or standing with one foot on a chair, helps gentle exploration of the vaginal opening.
- The wrapper should be removed and the tampon gently pushed upwards at a backwards angle into the vaginal opening as far as it will go comfortably. This should not hurt. Don't worry: it's very unlikely the tampon will get lost inside you.
- The withdrawal cord hangs down outside the body, for easy removal.

# Periods

## ADVANTAGES IN WEARING PADS

- They readily absorb blood as it leaves the body from the vaginal opening.
- The looped towels, used together with a sanitary belt, remain in the right place to catch the blood flow.
- Slim towels can be quite discreet, especially the press-on type.

## DISADVANTAGES IN WEARING PADS

- The loop towels in particular tend to be rather bulky and therefore cannot be used with confidence when wearing tight trousers, as you may be able to see the outline of the pad.
- They can be inconvenient especially when swimming or during sport.
- The towels may chafe the top of the legs, leaving them sore.
- Press-on towels sometimes move about, so blood may leak.

Towels should be changed every four hours, however light the blood flow. Although menstrual blood is clean and perfectly healthy, once outside the body it meets bacteria from the air and can cause a smell, which is obviously embarrassing. A daily wash or bath can help keep smells at bay. Soap can make the vagina sting and water is all that is necessary to keep it clean. Girls should wash their genitals from front to back to avoid spreading germs from the anus into the vagina.

## WHERE TO DISPOSE OF TOWELS

Look for the towels which say 'flushable' on the packet. Others may not flush and therefore block the toilet. If you have to dispose of them in some other way, then wrap them up securely in newspaper and put them in a dustbin. In public toilets you will normally find that bags and bins are provided.

## ADVANTAGES IN USING TAMPONS

- Once in place, the tampon cannot be felt.
- They are ideal to wear with tight-fitting trousers.
- You can have a bath, shower or go swimming with the tampon in.
- They are far more discreet and easier to carry around than towels.
- They are easily disposed of.

## DISADVANTAGES IN USING TAMPONS

- Some girls might forget they are wearing a tampon and leave it in for longer than the recommended six hours; it will then smell.
- If a tampon should get lost inside your vagina (this is rare) don't hesitate in going to your doctor.

Although there are advantages and disadvantages in using either tampons or pads, it is a personal decision depending on what is available.

# Skin, Hair and Hygiene

Puberty can be a troublesome time for skin. Spots are one of the biggest problems for any adolescent to cope with. The reason why they often appear during puberty is the change in hormone levels, which encourages the sebaceous glands in your skin to work overtime. In doing so, they produce an excess amount of sebum (an oily substance which coats both your hair and skin, keeping them supple and waterproof). With these glands being in great quantity over your face, neck and back, obviously these are the most likely places for spots to erupt. Various other types of blemish are also likely.

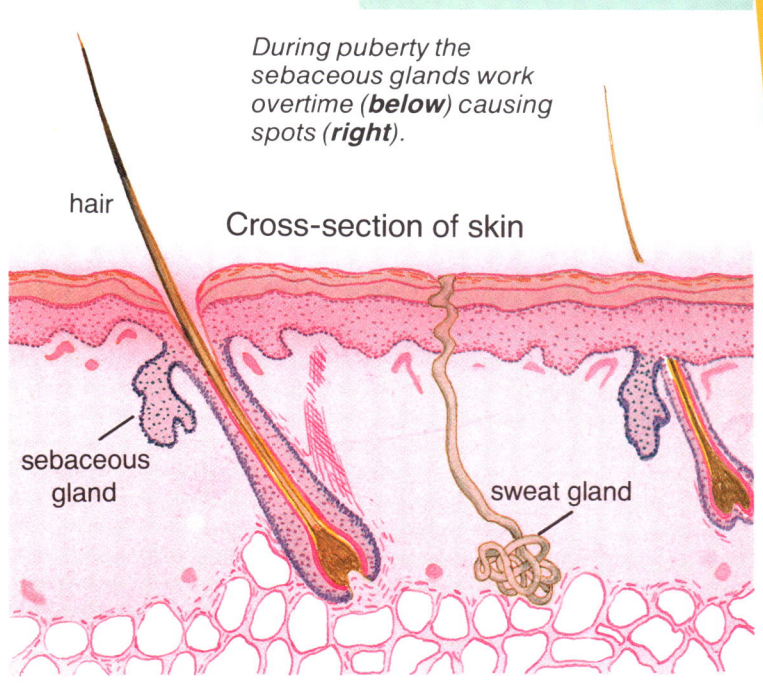

*During puberty the sebaceous glands work overtime (**below**) causing spots (**right**).*

hair

Cross-section of skin

sebaceous gland

sweat gland

## ACNE

An extremely common complaint amongst adolescents, both male and female, acne is neither a disease nor an infection but it is a problem for those suffering from it. Acne is caused by a buildup of sebum and its severity depends on the level of sex hormones you have in your blood and the degree of sensitivity of your sebaceous glands. But there is no need for anyone to suffer in silence: there are many preparations which your doctor can supply. There is some comfort: as long as you follow a sensible eating plan and keep your skin clean by using an antiseptic soap, acne can be cured. Most people simply grow out of it.

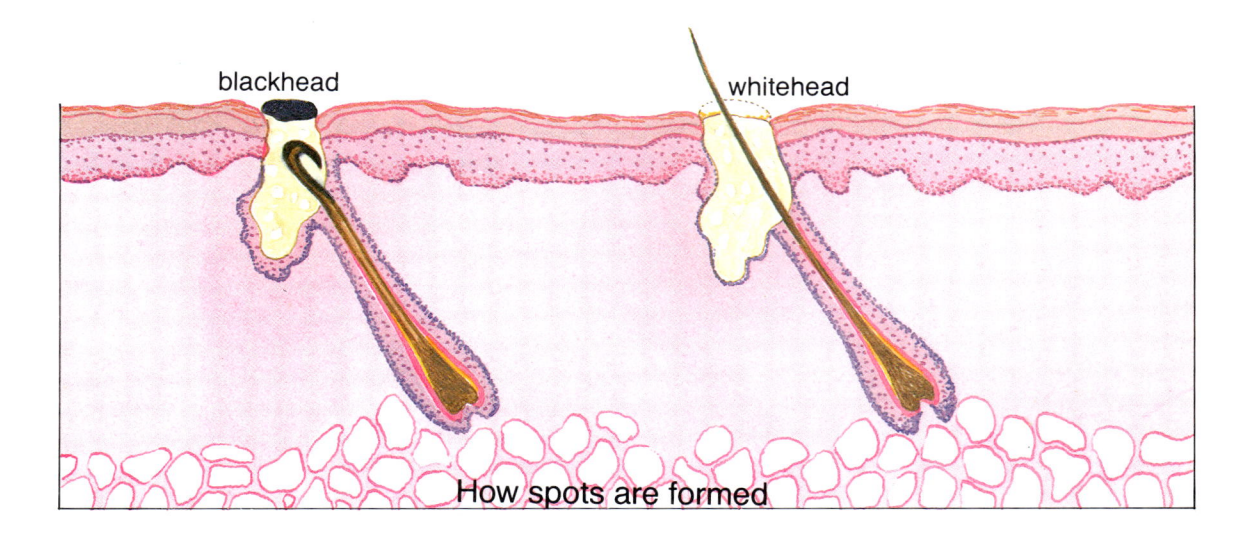

How spots are formed

## BLACKHEADS

These can be a real nuisance and are caused by sebum gathering at the opening of a sebaceous gland.

## WHITEHEADS

Whiteheads are caused by sebum building up below the surface of the sebaceous gland.

## DEALING WITH SPOTS

- Wash your face using a mild soap (preferably not perfumed).
- Don't use greasy make-up.
- Cut down on chips, chocolate, fatty foods.
- Drink plenty of water.
- Eat plenty of fresh fruit and vegetables.
- Never squeeze spots: infection can easily spread if hands are the slightest bit dirty.

## BOYS' SPOTS V GIRLS' SPOTS

As the hormone testosterone is more commonly involved with the formation of spots and males produce more of this hormone, boys do tend to have more problems with spots than girls do.

*Washing with a mild, unperfumed soap can help prevent spots.*

## SKIN TYPES

There are three basic types of skin: dry, oily and combination.

## DRY SKIN

Dry skin looks dry and sometimes flakes. It feels 'tight' if you wash it with soap and water. If you have dry skin, you are less likely to get spots than if you have oily skin but it can feel rough and uncomfortable. It may help if you stop using perfumed soap on your face. You can try using an unperfumed type or a cleansing cream instead. Skin will feel less 'tight' if moisturizing cream is used.

## OILY SKIN

Oily skin looks a bit shiny and it is often prone to spots. It doesn't dry out easily and does attract more dirt than dry skin. Soap and water or cleansers can be used to clean oily skin.

## COMBINATION SKIN

Most people have this skin type, with an oily patch in the centre of the face across the forehead, nose and chin, and dry cheeks. Dry areas can be moisturized after washing and oily patches treated as above.

*Top* Too much sun is bad for your skin.

**Right** Cleansers are more gentle than soap for dry skin.

▶ ▶ ▶ ▶ ▶ ▶ ▶ ▶ ▶ ▶ ▶ ▶ ▶ ▶ ▶

## SUN-TANNING

Although a sun-tan looks nice and makes you feel healthy, the ultraviolet rays in sunshine are harmful to the skin. Besides burning and sunstroke the long-term damage can be prematurely wrinkled skin. Once this happens, there is nothing you can do about it.

If you have light skin but feel you must have a tan, always use the right protective creams for your skin type and follow instructions carefully. Fair skins generally burn easily, black skins do not, and dark skins tan fairly easily.

## PERSONAL HYGIENE

From being young children, we are taught the importance of keeping ourselves clean. But it is more important than ever to keep your body clean and fresh during puberty, mainly because your skin starts producing more of the substances which cause unpleasant and offensive smells.

## SWEAT

During puberty we sweat more, especially under the arms and around the genital area. That is why it is important to have a shower or a top-to-toe wash every day. Not only does a thorough wash make you feel much better, it also relieves the body of its dead skin and sweat.

## BODY ODOUR (BO)

If you have ever had the misfortune to sit next to someone with BO (body odour), then you will know how quickly you wanted to get away from their company! Although it is part and parcel of the body's cooling down system, sweat has no smell as such. The smell comes from bacteria breaking down on the body and will remain until this is removed by washing. Deodorants or antiperspirants can be

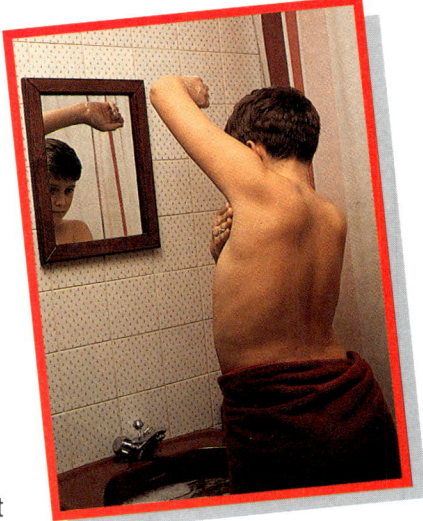

used under the arms. Deodorant contains chemicals which stop the sweat from smelling; antiperspirant stops the wetness.

## HAIR

The hormonal changes in your body during adolescence can also

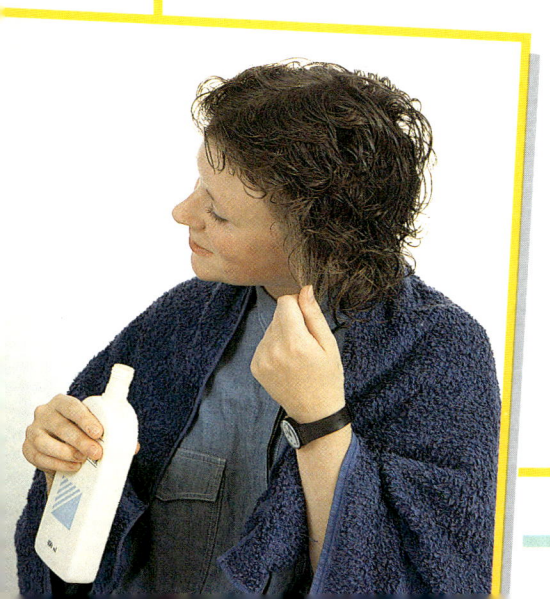

affect your hair. People with oily skin generally have oily hair while those with dry skin have dry hair.

## OILY HAIR

Often during puberty, the scalp produces more oil than usual, making hair look lank and sticky. Use a mild shampoo and avoid brushing or touching your hair a great deal, as this stimulates the glands into producing more oil.

## DRY HAIR

Dry hair gets tangled easily and feels dry to touch.

It happens if your scalp is producing less sebum than it should. Wash it about once every four days with a mild shampoo, followed by conditioner. Avoid combing hair when it is wet, as this can stretch it and split the ends.

## DANDRUFF

Dandruff is scales of skin which have accumulated on the surface of the scalp. If there is a lot of dandruff, try using a special shampoo for this and wash brushes and combs at the same time.

# Worries and Fears

While having to cope with the physical changes that are going on during puberty, there are also emotional changes to contend with. Hormones are responsible for these to some extent. Mood swings are extremely common during this time: one moment everything is going along fine, then the next moment, for no apparent reason, you feel down in the dumps. You may feel like screaming; you might want to throw all your clothes into the dustbin; you might want to sit down and have a good cry; you might want to laugh hysterically; you might think you are going mad but you're not. It is all part of growing up. This book deals with some of these worries and fears as they relate to your body. (More information on this in *Moods and Feelings*.)

Many questions not covered here are dealt with in other books in the series. For example, parents' reactions to your development are covered in *Family and Friends*.

◄◄◄◁

*Hormones are partly responsible for the mood changes in adolescence.*

### EARLY/LATE DEVELOPMENT

As you grow up, it is inevitable that you compare yourself with others. This can lead to worries about whether you are developing 'normally'. As we have seen, there are wide variations in the rate of development during puberty. While the average age for a girl to start her periods may be around twelve and a half, for example, ten or sixteen would still be normal.

However, both early and late development can be worrying for the person concerned. Girls who develop earlier than their friends can feel self-conscious and isolated, experiencing worries they cannot share, such as how to cope with periods. Boys who develop early do not normally face the same isolation. Their increased size and strength leads to improved sports skills, which their friends will probably admire.

Late development is worrying for both sexes, but particularly for boys who may be teased about their bodies. Both sexes can feel left out and fear they are abnormal. The age at which puberty starts really does not have an effect on adult sexual development, however. If you still feel worried, try to talk to someone sympathetic whom you can trust.

## GIRLS' WORRIES

One of the most common concerns for girls during adolescence is the size of their breasts. They either feel they are too flat-chested or over-developed. However, any size of breast is equally attractive, sensitive and capable of feeding a baby. Some nipples turn inwards but this does not prevent breast feeding.

Another worry is body shape: girls often feel they are too fat or thin, dislike the shape of their legs, or the build of their bodies. Magazine and television images make us all feel that we should look perfect. In reality we have to accept that we are what we are. While you can make the most of what you have through exercise and healthy eating, if you are small it is pointless wishing you were as tall as your friend. In fact, if you ask her, she probably wishes she were smaller!

*Above* Models on television make us feel that beauty means being slim and tall. *Left* In reality people of all sizes are attractive.

## BOYS' WORRIES

Boys often worry about the size of their penis. They may think it is too small or too big. All sizes are capable of making love and giving sexual pleasure.

In addition, erections can be embarrassing. They are usually triggered by something sexual, like seeing an attractive girl, but can happen at other times too. Often boys wake up with an erection, even if they have not been dreaming about sex.

Whilst a boy's body is still getting used to his hormonal changes, he may experience 'wet dreams'. These happen when a boy is sleeping. He has an erection and some semen spurts from his penis. Wet dreams happen during dreaming, although not necessarily about sex.

## AWKWARDNESS

As well as the body changes we have already discussed in this book, there are many invisible changes during puberty. For example, the heart's weight almost doubles, the lungs grow and blood pressure alters. Together with the more obvious changes, this can leave you feeling rather uncomfortable in your own body. You may feel clumsy and awkward in your movements as you learn to adjust.

**Above** *You may feel awkward and clumsy during adolescence.*
**Left** *Magazines often make girls feel unhappy with their looks.*

## SHYNESS

During adolescence we often become very self-conscious about our bodies and how other people view them. Some people react to this by wanting to show off their new adult shape. Others may feel very shy and want to disguise the fact that their shape is changing. Embarrassment at the sight of other people being naked, for example your parents, is also common. This is all quite normal and part of becoming independent and separate from our parents.

## TIME ALONE

As your body is going through the changes we have discussed in this book, you will probably find you need more time alone. You may want to examine yourself in the mirror, write a diary, listen to music or just have time to think. It is important that you have the privacy to do this. However, this can sometimes be difficult. Parents may worry what you are doing alone for so long, or brothers and sisters may want to intrude. Try explaining to your parents that you need to be alone and hopefully they will agree to keep other children out of your way.

**Top** Some people wear baggy clothes to disguise their changing shape.

**Below** Privacy and time alone are important during adolescence.

## HELP

If you need further advice on any of the topics covered here, there are useful addresses and a reading list at the back of this book. Remember, it always helps to talk to someone about your problems. If you cannot talk to your parents or teacher, choose someone whom you can trust or ring one of the help-line numbers in the further information section of this book.

# Glossary

**ACNE**
Inflammation of the sebaceous glands in the skin, a problem very common among adolescents. It is due to a change in their hormones.

**ADOLESCENCE**
Period between childhood and adulthood when the body undergoes many physical and emotional changes.

**AMENORRHOEA**
Absence of periods.

**ANTIPERSPIRANT**
Substance normally used under the arms to prevent too much sweating. It works by shutting off some of the pores.

**AREOLA**
Area around the nipple.

**CERVIX**
Neck of the uterus (womb).

**CIRCUMCISION**
Cutting off of the foreskin, done in many cultures for religious reasons.

**CLITORIS**
Small part of the female genitals, sensitive to touch.

**DEODORANT**
Used under the arms to prevent smells.

**DEPILATORY CREAM**
Cream used to remove unwanted hair.

**EPIDIDYMIS**
Small, coiled tube lying behind each testis.

**FALLOPIAN TUBES**
The two tubes which carry the egg cells from the ovaries to the uterus (womb).

**FERTILIZATION**
When the male sperm and female egg cells meet.

**FORESKIN**
Loose skin covering the end of the penis.

**FSH (FOLLICLE STIMULATING HORMONE)**
Hormone which stimulates egg production in ovaries.

**GENITALS**
External sex organs.

**GLANS**
Tip of the penis.

**GROWTH SPURT**
Time during puberty when your height increases very quickly.

**HORMONES**
Substance produced in the body and carried round in the bloodstream.

**HYMEN**
Thin layer of skin protecting the entrance to a girl's vagina.

**HYPOTHALAMUS**
Tiny part of the brain, one job of which is to trigger off puberty.

**LABIA**
Outer lips of the vagina.

**LH (LUTEINIZING HORMONE)**
Hormone which causes ovulation.

**MENOPAUSE**
Time when a woman stops having periods.

**MENSTRUAL CYCLE**
Length of time between one period and the next. A cycle is normally about twenty-eight days.

**MENSTRUATION**
Discharge of blood from the uterus which normally occurs in females from puberty until middle age.

**OVARIES**
Two organs in females which produce eggs.

**OVULATION**
Release of an egg from one of the ovaries, usually every four weeks or so, between periods.

# Glossary

**OVUM**
Female egg capable of growing into a baby if fertilized with a male sperm (ova is the plural).

**PELVIS**
Bones protecting the internal sexual organs.

**PENIS**
Male sexual organ.

**PERIODS**
See menstruation.

**PITUITARY GLAND**
Tiny gland at the base of the brain, which plays an important part in human growth and development.

**PMT (PREMENSTRUAL TENSION)**
Group of symptoms related to the menstrual cycle which can often make the days before a period rather unpleasant.

**PROSTAGLANDIN**
Hormone which triggers off labour and causes the uterus to contract.

**PROSTATE GLAND**
Small gland in the male body which produces a fluid enabling the sperm to move.

**PUBERTY**
Time when a young person's body is changing physically in readiness for adulthood.

**PUBIC HAIR**
Hair that grows around the genital areas.

**SANITARY TOWEL**
A piece of material used to catch blood during a period.

**SCROTUM**
Pouch of skin which holds the testicles.

**SEBACEOUS GLANDS**
Glands under the skin's surface, which produce sebum.

**SEBUM**
Oily substance which protects hair and skin.

**SEMEN**
Thick, whitish mixture of sperm and fluid which comes out of the penis.

**SEMINAL VESICLES**
Glands which produce a fluid to give energy to the sperm.

**SPERM**
Male cell, capable of fertilizing a female egg.

**TESTES/TESTICLES**
Male reproductive organs where sperm is produced and stored.

**TESTOSTERONE**
Hormone produced in the testicles responsible for male bodily changes during puberty.

**URETHRA**
Tube which has two functions: to carry urine out of the body in both sexes, and in boys to carry semen when the penis is sexually excited.

**URINE**
Fluid waste passed out of the urethra.

**UTERUS**
See womb.

**VAGINA**
Passage leading from the vulva to the womb in girls.

**VULVA**
External part of the female's genitals.

**WOMB**
Also known as the uterus. Large pear-shaped organ in females, in which a baby grows.

# Teachers' notes

You may find it useful to use the questions set out below as a basis for discussion or written work.

**From Child into Adolescent:** The vast number of physical changes during puberty can leave you feeling awkward and clumsy. Write a brief description of an experience which made you aware that your body was changing.

**Height and Shape:** The age at which puberty begins varies enormously. What reasons can you think of for this?
Do you think we are too affected by ideas of shape presented in the media?

**Body Hair:** Compare attitudes towards body hair in your culture with attitudes in another culture. Why do you think body hair is sometimes removed?

**Sexual Changes:** What do you think is the best way for people of your age to learn about sexual changes during puberty? Whose responsibility is it to teach you about this? For example, is it better to learn about periods and wet dreams at school, at home, or somewhere else?

**Periods:** What myths have you heard about periods?
Do you think that boys understand the difficulties girls have with periods?

**Skin, Hair and Hygiene:** Write a list of questions about the body that we have not answered in this book.

**Worries and Fears:** What sort of worries and fears do you think people have during adolescence?

# Books to read

*Everygirl's Lifeguide* by Miriam Stoppard (Dorling Kindersley 1987)

*Facts of Life: Growing Up* by Susan Meredith (Usborne 1985)

*It's More Than Sex* by Suzie Hayman (Wildwood House 1986)

*Make It Happy, Make It Safe* by Jane Cousins (Penguin 1988)

*The Royal Society of Medicine: Growing Up – A Guide for Children and Parents* by Dr James Doherty (Modus Books 1986)

# Acknowledgements

Allsport 24; Barnaby's Picture Library cover (bottom right); J Allan Cash 35, 38; Cephas 14, 27; Chapel Studios 8; Sally & Richard Greenhill cover (top and bottom left), 5, 33; Network 13 (bottom); Tim Woodcock 6 (left); Tim Woodcock/WPL 6 (right), 7, 11, 13 (top and centre), 17 (top and bottom), 26, 28, 29, 34, 36 (top), 37, 39 (right and left), 40 (top and bottom); WPL 35 (bottom), 36 (bottom).

Artwork: Clive Goodyer (cover); Pat Ludlow 10–11, 15, 21, 31, 38; Malcolm S. Walker 8–9, 12, 16, 18, 20, 22, 25, 30, 33, 34.

# Further information

**UK ADDRESSES**
These organizations can help you
wherever you live:

Alateen
61 Great Dover Street
London SE1 4YF
Tel. 01–403–0888
Glasgow: 041–2217356
Belfast: 0232–243489
*Alateen helps teenagers who have
relatives or friends with a drink problem.*

Children's Legal Centre
20 Compton Terrace
London N1 2UN
Tel. 01–359–9392
*Free advice on the law as it affects
children and young people.*

Contact Youth Counselling Service
2a Ribble Street
Newtownards Road, Belfast
Tel. 0232–57848
*Youth counselling service.*

Family Planning Information Service
27–35 Mortimer Street
London W1N 7RJ
Tel. 01–636–7866
*Information on sexual relationships and
contraception.*

Gay Switchboard
Tel. 01–837–7324
*Help for homosexual men and women.*

The Incest Crisis Line
32 Newbury Close
Northolt, Middlesex
Tel. 01–422–5100
*Counselling for incest victims; run by
incest victims.*

Rape Crisis Centre
Tel. 01–837–1600
*Counselling for women who have been
raped or sexually abused.*

Scottish Drug Forum
266 Clyde Street
Glasgow
Scotland G1 4JH
Tel. 041–221–1175
*Advice on drug abuse.*

SCODA
1–4 Hatton Place
Hatton Garden
London EC1N 8ND
Tel. 01–430–2341
*Information on drug abuse.*

Young Group of Gamblers Anonymous
17–23 Blantyre Street
London SW10
Tel. 01–352–3062
*Help for young people with a gambling
problem.*

In addition you may be able to find nearby
branches of the following organizations in
your telephone directory:
Alcoholics Anonymous *(for people with
drink problems)*
Brook Advisory Centres *(for information on
sex, abortion, pregnancy and other
problems)*
Family Planning Clinics *(for information on
contraception and pregnancy)*
Samaritans *(for the suicidal)*

# Further information

## AUSTRALIA ADDRESSES
The following give information on contraception and pregnancy:

Action Centre
268 Flinders Lane
Melbourne
Victoria 3000

Second Storey
Second Floor
102 Rundle Mall
Adelaide SA 500

The Warehouse
Penrith Youth Health Centre
20 Belmore Street
Penrith NSW 2750

## CANADA ADDRESSES
Abortion Outreach Centre
219 Dufferin Street
Toronto
(416) 535–5135
*For information about abortion.*

Aid to Women
411 Richmond Street East
Toronto
(416) 363–2325
*For information about pregnancy and abortion.*

Bellwood Health Services
1020 McNicoll
Toronto
(416) 495–0926
*For information about drug addiction and treatment.*

Kids' Help Line
(800) 668–6868
*For counselling on any topic.*

## NEW ZEALAND ADDRESSES
Family Planning Association
214 Karangahape Road
Auckland
Tel. 798–240

Help
Friendship House
Manukau City
Auckland
Tel. 277–9324

Rape Crisis Centre
63 Ponsonby Road
Ponsonby
Auckland
Tel. 764–404

Youthline
Tel. 797–888

## USA ADDRESSES
National Association of People with AIDS
2025 I Street NW
Suite 415
Washington DC 20006

National Child Abuse Hotline
Tel. 1–800–422–4453

National Gay Task Force
80 Fifth Avenue
New York
NY 10011
AIDS Hotline: Tel. 1–800–221–7044

National Runaway Hotline
Tel. 1–800–621–4000

Planned Parenthood Clinic
Tel. 1–800–223–3303